The Best Baking Matters

Gluten Free Dairy Free Recipes

By Heidi Baker

Copyright © 2013 by Heidi Baker
All rights reserved. Published in the United States by Heidi Baker. No part of this book may be reproduced in any manner whatsoever without prior written permission, except in the case of brief quotations embodied in critical articles or reviews. Your support of the author is truly appreciated.

Front cover designed by Heather Luxion. Back cover designed by Heidi Baker.

Dedication and Gratitude

I dedicate The Best of Baking Bakers Gluten Free Dairy Free Recipes to my mom, Helen N Katz (1945 – 2012). She was the label maker, babysitter and general administrator of Baking Bakers. Without her encouragement and help I never would have attempted to make a business out of one of my favorite pastimes. As far as I'm concerned she's still the Head Administrator with an office in the sky.

Table of Contents

Introduction 6

Almond Butter (or Cashew Butter) Chocolate Chip Brownies 8

Chocolate Lovers' Chocolate Cake 10

Chocolate Frosting 11

"White" Cake (variations listed below recipe)* 12

"White" Frosting – option one 13

"White" Frosting – option two 13

Chocolate Chip Banana Bread 14

Vegan Banana (Walnut) Bread 15

Pumpkin Bread 16

Vegan Apple-Cinnamon or Blueberry Muffins 17

Basic Cookie (variations listed below recipe)* 18

White Bread 20

Garlic bread 22

Brown Bread 24

Introduction

You now have in your hands the results of two years of obsessive baking and recipe creating. Most of my friends can eat gluten all day, but the goodies I make are so yummy, a good percentage of them have asked me for recipes for their own enjoyment and to please bring an Orange-Cinnamon Cake, a pan of Brownies, a batch of Almond Cookies, a loaf of Garlic Bread, etc. to the next gathering. Here's how it all began.

In the spring of 2008, through the process of elimination and reintroduction (more than once for I didn't want to believe what was happening), I knew that gluten was causing me to have digestive discomfort akin to labor pains. At the time I was already used to baking from scratch; I only used organic whole wheat flour, sucanat or organic sugar and I adapted most recipes to be non-dairy for my nieces. Still, I was intimidated by having to learn how to bake with new and mysterious flours.

Once I decided to stop trying to find forms of gluten I could digest properly, I boldly marched into Whole Foods and picked up a gluten-free chocolate cake mix. I was mostly impressed. It made a real cake, but there was a certain something not quite right. I took one of these first gluten-free cakes to a potluck. It was well received by more than half the people gathered, which was encouraging, but unacceptable. Half is too few. I like the approval of three quarters or more, at least one "Mmmmm, mmmmm, mmmmm!" and a "Can I get that recipe from you?" It would be another year before I got serious about meeting that goal with my own gluten-free recipes.

The real baking adventures began when my friend Sandra and I started baking together in Winter 2009. She enjoys baking and a challenge so jumped right in to figuring out how to help me make gluten-free goodies that were delicious on their own merit rather than passable-considering-the-wheat-was-missing.

Early on I had the unproductive habit of making adaptations to a recipe idea fairly in midair. I never wrote down what I was adding more or less of, or what I was omitting altogether. After a few weeks of mounting confusion, as I seemed unable to make the same recipe twice (go figure), and Sandra politely suggesting I note the changes, she obtained pen, paper, my attention and kindly wrote down every adaptation until I decided she had a good point and started taking responsibility for this aspect of recipe making. When I finally began keeping track of what we were learning, the process got really fun. Think Muppet scientists, flour flying, and cookies and muffins on almost every sticky surface.

Over time a transition occurred. Unsolicited, many friends and family, truly enjoying this untraditional food even though it wasn't normally *their thing,* suggested I either write a cookbook, sell my goodies, or both, because I was producing goods that were so good they needed to be shared, especially with folks who were limited by celiac or a gluten intolerance. As the pressure mounted, I realized that's exactly what I needed to do. So I am happy to offer this first "Bake Book" of easy-to-follow recipes nearly anyone is sure to love.

You can follow me on Facebook at "Baking Bakers, gluten free, Urbana Illinois."

Enjoy!

Almond Butter (or Cashew Butter) Chocolate Chip Brownies

Preheat oven to 350 degrees.

> 1 16 oz jar smooth almond butter (no salt or added oils) or cashew butter*
> 2 large eggs
> 1 ¼ cups Sucanat or Coconut sugar or Organic sugar
> ½ cup almond or rice milk
> ½ cup cocoa powder
> 1 tsp. gluten-free vanilla extract
> ½ tsp. salt
> 1 tsp. baking soda
> 1 cup Enjoy Life chocolate chips
> -OR-
> 1 bar of an Organic Fair Trade chocolate bar broken in small pieces (or other brand)

In large bowl, dump almond butter. Mix with hand mixer on low/med speed until smooth, then add each ingredient in order, mixing after each addition. (Salt and baking soda can be added together). Manually mix in cocoa powder before turning mixer back on in order to avoid a big cocoa puff all over the counter.

Spread evenly in oiled 13x9x2-inch cake pan. Bake for 36 minutes. Let cool for at least 15 minutes (if you can).

Variations: Organic Fair Trade chocolate bars come in several varieties, like Dark Chocolate Orange or Mint. Endangered species brand has several good chocolate bars as well.

My favorite for these brownies is Toffee Crunch, which does have a small amount of dairy. If dairy is not an issue, I highly recommend trying this adaptation.

*This afternoon, (as the store was out of almond butter) I made Cashew Butter Brownies by substituting a 16oz jar of Once Again Cashew Butter (containing cashews and sunflower oil) in place of the almond butter. I was very happy with the result. I took the pan of brownies to a gathering. The response was one rave review *after another. I've only made them this once and had to punt when I realized I only had a bit over a ¼ cup of cocoa powder. So I added ground bakers chocolate made in a dedicated coffee grinder. For this reason, I can't say for sure they'll come out just as yummy with the intended ½ cup of cocoa powder (though I think they will), but I wanted to add the variation to this first book just in case someone out there can eat cashews but not almonds and would appreciate knowing about this possible substitution.*

Chocolate Lovers' Chocolate Cake

Preheat oven to 350 degrees.

Mix well in large bowl

> 1 cup Bob's Red Mill gluten-free all purpose baking flour
> ¾ cup millet flour
> 1 ½ cups organic coconut sugar
> ¾ cup cocoa powder
> 3 Tbsp. flax meal
> 1 ½ tsp. gluten-free baking powder
> 1 ½ tsp. baking soda
> 1 tsp. salt

Then add

> ½ cup grapeseed oil
> 2 cups + 2 Tbsp. rice milk
> 1 tsp. gluten-free vanilla extract
> 3 eggs
> 1 "flax egg"*

Mix well

Pour batter into oiled 13x9x2-inch cake pan.

Bake 27 – 30 minutes. Once toothpick comes out basically clean, it's done.

*One "flax egg" = combine 1 Tbsp. flax meal with 3 Tbsp. rice milk. Barely simmer, either on the stovetop or in the microwave. Remove from heat, whip with fork. Put in fridge for a few minutes. Once cool, whip again with fork and add to recipe.

Let cake cool completely before adding frosting.

Chocolate Frosting

Mash together into semi-solid mass

>1 cup powdered coconut sugar (can be powdered in a dedicated coffee grinder)
>1 cup Spectrum palm oil (do NOT soften with heat)

Then add and mash in until well combined

>¾ cup cocoa powder
>½ cup rice milk
>1 tsp. gluten-free vanilla extract

Mix with hand mixer for approximately 2 – 4 minutes or until smooth. (At first, when you start mixing it will look all wrong. But after a short while it gets very smooth and beautiful).

"White" Cake
(variations listed below recipe)*

Preheat oven to 350 degrees.

In mixing bowl, combine

>1 ¼ cups Bob's Red Mill all purpose gluten-free flour
>¾ cup sucanat or coconut sugar
>1 ½ tsp. gluten-free baking powder
>½ tsp. salt

then add

>½ cup grapeseed oil or other vegetable oil
>1 tsp. gluten-free vanilla extract
>3 large eggs
>½ cup coconut milk (full fat's best) or rice or almond milk

Mix well.

Pour into oiled 8x8-inch cake pan, bake for 30 – 35 minutes. Remove from oven as soon as toothpick comes out clean.

Let cake cool completely before adding frosting.

*The recipe as written is a simple white cake (tan actually, since our ingredients have naturally occurring color) The cake can be flavored any way you like, same with the frosting.

I especially enjoy Cinnamon-orange cake with Lemon frosting: add 1 ½ tsp. cinnamon to dry and 1 tsp. gluten-free orange extract once wet ingredients are added.

For frosting (on next page) add 1 to 1 ½ tsp. gluten-free lemon extract.

The possibilities are endless.

"White" Frosting – option one

In medium bowl, mash together

> 1 cup Spectrum palm oil (do NOT heat to soften)
> 2 cups Organic powdered sugar

then add

> 2 Tbsp. rice milk
> ½ tsp. gluten-free vanilla extract
> 3 Tbsp. agave nectar or maple syrup

Mix with electric beater until desired consistency.

"White" Frosting – option two

In a medium bowl, mash together 1 cup Spectrum palm oil (do NOT heat to soften) and 1 cup plus 1 Tbsp. powdered coconut sugar (powdered by grinding coconut sugar in a dedicated coffee grinder).

This step takes a bit of time, but it will come together.

Once fairly well combined, add 2 Tbsp. rice, almond or coconut milk.

Then get out the hand mixer and blend until smooth.

Chocolate Chip Banana Bread

Preheat oven to 325 degrees.

Mash together in large bowl

> 2 bananas (1 ¼ cups mashed)
> ¼ cup grape seed oil or other vegetable oil

Then add and mix in well

> 2 eggs
> ½ cup organic agave nectar or maple syrup

Then add and mix in well

> 1 tsp. baking soda
> pinch of salt

In a separate bowl, combine

> 1 cup Bob's Red Mill all purpose gluten-free baking flour
> ½ cup Bob's Red Mill sweet white rice flour

Pour dry into wet and mix well

> stir in 1/3-1/2 cup Enjoy Life chocolate chips

Pour equal amounts of batter into *three* 3x5-inch oiled bread pans.

Bake 24 to 28 minutes (until toothpick comes out clean).

Remove from pans and set on cooling rack. If needed, run a plastic knife around edges and corners for ease of loaf removal. If you don't have a cooling rack, a plate will suffice.

Vegan Banana (Walnut) Bread

Preheat oven to 325 degrees.

Mash together in large bowl

>2 bananas (1 ¼ cups mashed)
>¼ cup grape seed oil or other vegetable oil

Then add and mix in well

>2 "flax eggs"*
>½ cup organic agave nectar or maple syrup

Then add and mix well

>1 tsp. baking soda
>pinch of salt

In a medium bowl combine

>1 cup Bob's Red Mill all purpose gluten-free baking flour
>½ cup Bob's Red Mill sweet white rice flour

Add dry to wet, mix well

>stir in ½ cup chopped walnuts (optional)

Pour equal amounts of batter into *three* 3x5-inch oiled bread pans.

Bake 24 to 28 minutes (until toothpick comes out clean).

Remove from pans and set on cooling rack. If needed, run a plastic knife around edges and corners for ease of loaf removal.

*Two "flax eggs" = combine 2 Tbsp. flax meal with 6 Tbsp. rice or almond milk. Barely simmer, either on the stovetop or in the microwave. Remove from heat, whip with fork. Put in fridge for a few minutes. Once cool, whip again with fork and add to recipe.

Pumpkin Bread

Preheat oven to 325 degrees.

Combine in large bowl

> 1 cup canned pumpkin
> 1 ½ Tbsp rice or almond milk
> ¼ cup grape seed oil or other vegetable oil

Then add and mix in well

> 2 large eggs
> ½ cup organic agave nectar or maple syrup

Then add and mix in

> 1 tsp. baking soda
> pinch of salt

In medium bowl, mix together

> 1 cup Bob's Red Mill all purpose gluten-free baking flour
> ½ cup Bob's Red Mill sweet white rice flour
> 1 ½ tsp. cinnamon
> ½ tsp. ginger
> ½ tsp. nutmeg

Add dry to wet, combine well

> mix in 1/3 cup Enjoy Life chocolate chips *or* ½ cup walnut pieces at this point (optional)

Pour into *three* 3x5-inch oiled bread pans.

Bake 25 to 30 minutes, until toothpick comes out clean.

Remove from pans and set on cooling rack. If needed, run a plastic knife around edges and corners for ease of loaf removal.

Vegan Apple-Cinnamon or Blueberry Muffins

Preheat oven to 350 degrees.

In large bowl, combine

> 2 cups Bob's Red Mill all purpose gluten-free baking flour
> ½ cup Arrowhead Mills gluten-free buckwheat flour
> 1 ½ tsp. baking soda
> 1 tsp. gluten-free baking powder
> 1 tsp. salt
> 3 Tbsp. flax meal
> 1 ½ tsp. cinnamon (only for apple cinnamon muffins)

Then add and mix well

> 2 "flax eggs"*
> 1 13.66 oz can Thai Kitchen coconut milk
> ½ cup rice or almond milk
> 1 cup agave nectar or maple syrup
> ½ cup Earth Balance margarine gently melted

Then gently stir in fruit**

> **Fruit variations

-Apple cinnamon: 2 cups diced apples and remember to add cinnamon with dry ingredients.
-Blueberry muffins: 1 ½ cups fresh blueberries *or* one 10oz bag of frozen blueberries, thawed and well drained

Fill oiled muffin tins about 2/3 full and bake 15 – 20 minutes.

Makes 16 – 18 muffins.

*Two "flax eggs" = combine 2 Tbsp. flax meal with 6 Tbsp. rice or almond milk. Barely simmer, either on the stovetop or in the microwave. Remove from heat, whip with fork. Put in fridge for a few minutes. Once cool, whip again with fork and add to recipe.

Basic Cookie
(variations listed below recipe)*

Preheat oven to 350 degrees.

In a medium bowl, mash together

>1 ¼ cups sucanat or organic sugar or coconut sugar
>½ cup spectrum palm oil
>½ cup grapeseed or other vegetable oil

Then add and mix well

>2 eggs *or* 2 "flax eggs"**
>3 Tbsp. rice or almond milk

In a second bowl, combine

>¾ cup almond flour
>1 cup Bob's Red Mill all purpose gluten-free baking flour
>½ cup coconut flour
>3 Tbsp. flax meal
>¼ tsp. salt
>¼ tsp. baking soda

Add wet mixture to dry, mix well.

Cover with foil and put in freezer for at least 20 minutes before baking. (More time in the freezer will not be a problem).

Line cookie sheet with parchment paper. Evenly space teaspoon-sized dollops onto cookie sheet. I use a teaspoon size ice-cream scoop for ease and uniformity, but a tsp. measure and a spoon work fine. Gently fatten each dollop into a circle.

Bake 11-12 minutes, or a couple minutes longer if you like crisper cookies. Cookies should begin to brown at the edges.

*The recipe as written will make a boring cookie. The magic comes in the variations.

I make Orange Chocolate Chip Cookies by adding 1½ to 2 tsp. gluten-free orange extract to the wet mixture and 2/3 cup Enjoy Life chocolate chips after the wet and dry are combined.

Almond-chocolate chip are very popular, as well as lemon-chocolate chip, plain orange, and plain almond. I've also added 1/3 cup of cocoa for especially chocolaty cookies, which works well, but I lessen the flour so I only use ¼ cup coconut and ½ cup almond flour.

Sometimes I reduce the coconut and almond flours by ¼ cup *each* (same as measurements for the cocoa-added variation, but without the cocoa of course) for a thinner, crispier, richer cookie. This variation should be made with eggs.

**Two "flax eggs" = combine 2 Tbsp. flax meal with 6 Tbsp. rice or almond milk. Barely simmer, either on the stovetop or in the microwave. Remove from heat, whip with fork. Put in fridge for a few minutes. When cool, whip again with fork and add to recipe.

White Bread

Whisk together in large bowl

    2 ¼ cups Jules gluten-free flour (available @ JulesGlutenFree.com)
    ¾ cup sorghum flour
    1 tsp. salt
    2 ½ tsp. yeast
    2 Tbsp. sucanat
    2 Tbsp. flax meal
    1 tsp. xanthan gum

Then add and mix in

    1 cup warm rice milk (120-125 degrees)

Then add and mix with fork until a more solid mass

    3 eggs
    5 Tbsp. Earth Balance margarine or butter
    1 tsp. Bragg's apple cider vinegar

Then mix with hand mixer using dough attachments, until "creamy."

With rubber spatula, pull batter from sides of bowl to form somewhat of a ball.

Let rise in bowl for 1 hour (less time in a really hot kitchen). Then transfer to oiled non-stick 8x4-inch bread pan, or *two* 3x5-inch oiled non-stick bread pans. Then cover with cellophane and let rise for 1 hour (less if kitchen is really hot).

Remove cellophane, bake in NON-preheated oven at 350 degrees for 44 minutes in 8x4-inch pan, 25 to 30 minutes in 3x5-inch pans. (When a toothpick comes out clean, bread is done).

Pop bread out of pans (If bread doesn't pop right out, use plastic knife around edges and corners to gently pull loaf away from sides).

Let cool one hour on cooling rack.

Your bread is ready to slice. I find that a sharp, straight-edge blade works best.

Garlic bread

Whisk together in large bowl

    2 ¼ cups Jules gluten-free flour (available @ JulesGlutenFree.com)
    ¾ cup millet flour
    1 tsp. salt
    2 ½ tsp. yeast
    2 Tbsp. sucanat
    2 Tbsp. flax meal
    1 tsp. xanthan gum
    2 tsp. garlic powder
    ½ tsp. oregano
    ½ tsp. basil

Then add and mix in

    1 cup warm rice milk (120-125 degrees)

Then add and mix with fork until a more solid mass

    3 eggs
    5 Tbsp. Earth Balance margarine or butter
    1 tsp. Bragg's apple cider vinegar

Then mix with hand mixer using dough attachments, until "creamy."

With rubber spatula, pull batter from sides of bowl to form somewhat of a ball.

Let rise in bowl for 1 hour (less time in a really hot kitchen). Then transfer to oiled non-stick 8x4-inch bread pan, or *two* 3x5-inch oiled non-stick bread pans.

Cover with cellophane and let rise for 1 hour (less if kitchen is really hot).

Remove cellophane, bake in NON-preheated oven at 350 degrees for 44 minutes in 8x4-inch pan, 25 to 30 minutes in 3x5-inch pans (when toothpick comes out clean, bread is done).

Pop bread out of pan (If bread doesn't pop right out, use plastic knife around edges and corners to gently pull loaf away from side).

Let cool one hour on cooling rack.

Your bread is ready to slice. I find a sharp, straight-edge blade works best.

Brown Bread

Whisk together in large bowl

    2 ¼ cups Jules gluten-free flour (available @ JulesGlutenFree.com)
    ¾ cup Arrowhead Mills gluten-free buckwheat flour
    ¼ cup coconut flour
    1 tsp. salt
    2 ½ tsp. yeast
    2 Tbsp. sucanat
    2 Tbsp. flax meal
    1 tsp. xanthan gum

Then add and mix in

    1 1/8 cup warm rice milk (120-125 degrees)

Then add and mix with fork until a more solid mass

    3 eggs
    5 Tbsp. Earth Balance margarine or butter
    ¼ cup agave nectar or maple syrup
    1 tsp. Bragg's apple cider vinegar

Then mix with hand mixer using dough attachments, until "creamy."

With rubber spatula, pull batter from sides of bowl to form somewhat of a ball.

Let rise in bowl for 1 hour (less time in a really hot kitchen). Then transfer to oiled non-stick 8x4-inch bread pan, or *two* 3x5-inch oiled non-stick bread pans.

Cover with cellophane and let rise for 1 hour (less if kitchen is really hot).

Remove cellophane, bake in NON-preheated oven at 350 degrees for 44 minutes in 8x4-inch pan, 25 to 30 minutes in 3x5-inch pans (when toothpick comes out clean, bread is done).

Pop bread out of pan (If bread doesn't pop right out, use plastic knife around edges and corners to gently pull loaf away from side).

Let cool one hour on cooling rack.

Your bread is ready to slice. I find a sharp, straight-edge blade works best.

Printed in Great Britain
by Amazon